D0613285

Praise for *A Fine Canopy*

"These poems thrive beneath a canopy of nuanced connections with crows, stars, leaves, lakes, a lover, a daughter, and most potently, a self. Swan offers us poems of faith and resilience that arise from her deep, sustained perception of a natural world where 'everything gives back light.'"

—Diane Seuss, author of *Four-Legged Girl* and
Still Life with Two Dead Peacocks and a Girl

"Thank all the muses that these beautiful poems by Alison Swan arrive to help us take notice of our own fragility and that of our world. Not oblivious to sorrow, far from it, but so raptly involved in all that constitutes the ground beneath our feet and the canopy above us as to give us heart. This book is truly restorative reading."

—Linda Gregerson, *Prodigal: New and Selected Poems*

"It makes sense that a terrain as extraordinary as the Great Lakes would find voice in a poet as glorious as Alison Swan. I am smitten. Swan writes with bone-deep passion, astonishing clarity, and watchful tending about life 'at the edge of a freshwater sea.' This collection is an almanac, a chronicle, a sacrificial offering to a particular landscape, and also a paean to all beings. The poems fly about with lives of their own, breathing inside their skins, beautiful and endangered."

—Janisse Ray, author of *Ecology of a Cracker Childhood*
and *A House of Branches: Poems*

"These poems offer us acts of attention and tenderness, two things we need now more than ever."

—Mary Ruefle, Vermont poet laureate and finalist
for the 2020 Pulitzer Prize for poetry

A
FINE
CANOPY

Made in Michigan Writers Series

GENERAL EDITORS

Michael Delp, Interlochen Center for the Arts
M. L. Liebler, Wayne State University

A complete listing of the books in this series can be found online at wsupress.wayne.edu

A FINE CANOPY

POEMS BY ALISON SWAN

WAYNE STATE UNIVERSITY PRESS
DETROIT

© 2020 by Alison Swan. All rights reserved. No part of this book may be reproduced without formal permission.

ISBN 978-0-8143-4806-2 (paperback)
ISBN 978-0-8143-4807-9 (e-book)

Library of Congress Control Number: 2020939005

Publication of this book was made possible by a generous gift from The Meijer Foundation.

Wayne State University Press
Leonard N. Simons Building
4809 Woodward Avenue
Detroit, Michigan 48201-1309

Visit us online at wsupress.wayne.edu

For Sophie

CONTENTS

1

2

3

4

1

After Reading *The Late, Great Lakes*

The dead gave their last blood to birds:
cardinals, red-winged blackbirds, and the downy woodpecker,
red-capped, persistent,

extracting food from trees in small portions
in every season. Deer browse fairways, medians, and kitchen gardens.
More real estate is parceled, so

more roads flood fields and woods.
Shores erupt in built things that have never held a seed.
And citylight falls over us like flames.

On the beach where waves arrive,
caddis worms gather forest litter into cloaks, then creep
almost invisible, into fresh water

where fish rise from the bottom and eat
what they need and when, a great lake flowing coolly over
them and under them and through.

Night Train

Because the train whistles
I know I am someplace

The sound becomes a perch in the air
where I wait for the sun

which has never known a train's
honed wheels on a polished track

except maybe as one of the sounds
the Earth makes as it marks the Milky Way

I am in a place I say and know it
the same way this glossy crow knows

earth and not earth and the tree between
Place to stand and place from which to leap

So absolutely ordinary we say as if we know
As if every single one of us knows

how to fly and when to fly and where
Think of feather vanes and snug skin

matter-of-fact ongoingness
which is maybe not matter-of-fact at all

Crows gather and watch or don't watch
Hop or fly or perch with gravity and feet

Things that hold earth and hold us to it
Some of the things that keep us home

Passerine

Talk about being a tree. How about the guy
standing behind the checkout counter at Dunham's,
ringing up sporting goods all day, twenty feet
from a wall of plate glass doors that admit sun, wind,
and the aura of hundreds of tons of vehicles gathered,
orderly, on a sea of asphalt. *Sea*, we say, as if,
and then walk through it insouciantly, wearing
nothing but clothing and jewelry.
Where are you most vulnerable? On foot,
at a busy intersection, five lanes of traffic
speeding in every direction and not a single light
that totally serves walkers. You must strategize
and take your chances. Laws must be passed
to give you the right of way. *Do not take on a car,*
I used to say to my beautiful husband in his
beautiful body. *You will not win.* And thus I
taught our daughter who seems to have been born
fearing things I've never had a chance to know.
Not so much passerine as car, world lurid
with color and light that serve automobiles, not
walkers or standers or ringer-uppers. You know
the drill: *Stay inside. Stay inside. Stay inside.*
Unless you're automobile. If you're auto, you
already know: we're remaking the world for you.
We're remaking the world for you and calling it good.
Keep the faith. Be patient. We are almost finished.

After an Elder Was Found in the Woods, Dead from a Self-Inflicted Gunshot

Scarlet needle threaded with birdsong
                    tugs the bower behind the family barn
          into these young woods

Frog captured and worried to death
                    between boy hands

Toad taken
        mistaken for Frog and drowned in a bucket

Snake caught
        controlled for one perfect day then released
                    back to the woodpile

Turtle watched from the riverbank who did not
                    the boy noted with something like pleasure
        watch him

Veery singing out of sight marking an overstory
                    the boy hadn't yet considered
        but would

Sneakers caked
        Jeans muddy at the knees
                    The sky a colossus

    O cardinal song then
                    O cardinal song now

Reading *Walden* Under a Thomas Wood Painting
After the Latest News About Drones

Sun cool as the moon
Moon impassive as mountains
Mountains weightless as clouds
Clouds still as mud
Mud clear as water
Water opaque as pebbles
Pebbles bright as stars

The Day After the Day After

Rather than send it to a landfill,
I carry a leftover dollop outside to the compost pile
and scrape it into the heap of leaves.

I pass back-porch pumpkin and driveway cairn.
Nuthatch flits from twig to twig in the crown of paw paw.
Sun beats down on all of us,

beats us into gold and silver,
even stone smoothed millennia ago by river
but only here at the surface of satellite Earth.

Yesterday, I walked out into not-quite-icy dawn,
emptyhanded in bare feet.
Maple straightened up and I waded in.

November 10, 2016

Grace

It has been subzero for days
and our house is snug,
sure, but I feel like I'm freezing.

The sky is blue. The snow is
blue, too. And if there's green
in those evergreens
I don't see it. Winter,
a hundred days long.

Midwinter, mid-Michigan
who doesn't love a cardinal,
something red and quick and loud?
How many Februaries have I
listened for their song?

The birds, who have sacrificed
so very much more than I,
float above the trees even today
when the cold is too cold for school.

The cedar hedge scatters sunlight
and I see palm fronds,
fuchsia bougainvillea,
that even the barest trees
serve birds.

Their hollow bones
make them lighter than air.
Their tiny hearts keep us all
from freezing.

Ground Watchers

Each morning Arturo
wanders his backyard,
the grassed and treed
rough on the other side
of the fence we share,
his family and mine.

Today I watched him
toddle. A single phoebe
and too-soon cardinal
leavened crow caws
I swear were absent from
the place where I was born.

I have made it this far
to perch in a shed, looking
out at old outbuildings,
train tracks, and a new boy
who watches the ground
unless he's running.

Down the hill the river
flows toward Lake Erie,
bits of this place suspended,
the leaf Arturo lifted up to
his eyes and nose, and
the leaf I swept from the walk.

What comes back upriver
and uphill? And how will
Arturo and I recognize it?
A fan of feathers across
the wings of a great blue
heron, its beak, its feet.

Bats Are Darker Than Dark Sky

A remnant
of brown velvet flies
as if it is just about to fall

more like a blown leaf
than a bird
forgetting to roost

cresting
our old spruce
darker than this dark sky

earth
the loamy kind
carried up and up

Back Country

I lie back under a hand-stitched painting
of flower blossoms, alone on sheets so white they
light up the dimmed hospital room. I'm afraid.
I'm afraid, so I think of loves, loves invited
and loves let go, especially the biggest love,
the love who touched the world first between these legs,
just as she began to leave me, a leaving
that feels like a light storm, brilliant white light that
makes me close my eyes when they should be open,
even walking outside in the daytime
under the great trees of our neighborhood, trees
that were saplings when I was twenty and trees
that are saplings now. I've only just begun
to consider my limbs, the way they've made
a gateway, held my daughter, carried my daughter;
the way they have held me up, carried me into
an unsettled mountain valley as cold rain
turned to snow, then snow cover revealed cougar
tracks, walking over them its own kind of coming home
to a house big and wild enough, a house that
felt as I entered it like a darker kind of storm.

Deep Dark

When I pause at the foot of a long driveway,
lights go on in the house and a door opens.

A whitish blur crosses the road,
then goes still upon the silver lawn.

Mae tugs the leash halfheartedly,
but neither of us wants to get any closer, not really,

not to the animal or the curious human,
each one of us writing, *Here I am*, onto the night

while leafy crowns transpire far above us and far below
the boundary between earth

and everything else that is. The moon's unrisen
or new. Stars mark patterns

older than anything we will ever be able to touch.
There has always only been this,

the winkings and workings of infinite atoms and quarks,
matter we now know speeds

through something akin to molasses or syrup,
not just gravity but literal cosmic drag.

What sort of life inures one to the relief
of knowing things we cannot see.

Outside

Snowplows pass on the road
She can feel them in her bones
like the vibration of the furnace
A ship's engine in the ship
of her house chugging through
swells so far out to sea there are
goddesses and nothing whatsoever
to fear from the dark

Neighbor

Days have passed and
they do not move

They do not walk into
the road after carkill

They do not hunch on
a branch and watch

They do not squawk and
they do not soar

Small bundle of
dark feathers on
the growing lawn

They do not soar and
they do not squawk

They do not hunch on
a branch and watch

They do not walk into
the road after carkill

They do not move and
days have passed

The Living

Two black crows work
at clearing the gray road

Their forage glistens

Our car is nearly
upon them
before they flap
four glossy wings

They enter the air
as if it is their palace

They cannot stay
there or here

Courage

If you're housecleaning
and shake a bat corpse
from among your things
please do us all a favor

Carry the little body
out of the house
and into the wide world

The world that shelters birds
and worms and bats

The world that animates
whatever building
you shelter in

Bury the bat in leaves at most
Eschew marker or prayer

And then be the tree that's ready
to wait for its forest

Here

Newportville holds us in the twigs of a nest for however many weeks a living thing takes to move itself out from under feathers and into leaves—at least that's the way it works here, where robins, jays, and wrens have fledged before our eyes.

In this neighborhood leaves still outnumber almost every other living thing. Crow caws and woodpecker taps have performed the bass line for at least six other birds at once, all of them soprano and certain—or so it seems, and for the happy shouts of the grandpa who lives in the house between ours and the river, and for the laughter of his grandson.

Here, it is the custom to leave the windows open, uncovered. The ingenious mesh makes a fine canopy. Sometimes a kind of carnival pours out. Sometimes a kind of carnival pours in.

2

The Dump at Ciudad Juárez

They left home because
they wanted to live

Now day and night the earth
on which they have built new walls
around their beds and chairs
family photos and statues of saints
shifts and shifts again

Sleep lowers mothers into putrid gaps
that swallow children
Mothers dream of trees
holding their sons and daughters high above it all
In dreams babies change to birds

Mothers lay their kitchen tables with meals
and invite their neighbors in
They offer drinks of water
They receive drinks of water
They are planting gardens

Pathways form in the dirt
new house to new house to new house

Everyone stands upright
pressing crowns hard into the clouds
Mothers lift and lower their wings
and lift them again
Roots work their way
through the waste

Snow

Snow as reminder of limits
> *water vapor frozen into hexagonal crystals*
> *that fall to earth in soft, white flakes and spread*
> *often upon it as white layer*

Snow as spackle
> flint
> dope
> emergency
> crime

Snow as the last thing we want to see come April

Snow as *fence, flake, goose,*
Snow as *-in-summer, job, leopard, line*

Snow as pantomime
> infinite
> artifact from another world

Snow as *there are not seventy Inuit words that's a myth*

Snow as relief
Snow as *isn't it amazing we get this much coverage*
> *when each flake is so small?*
Snow as reason to leave the house, finally
Snow as salve
> antidote
> cure
Snow as *we have never been so sure winter is*
> *better with it*
Snow as foundation
> insulation
> coverlet
Snow slipping toward
> slipping from dead trees I'm mourning

Snow as shroud

Snow as mantle
Snow as umbrella caught on hemlock twigs

Snow as *every flake different*
    vernacular
    water
    raw material of glaciers

Snow as anachronism
    relic
Snow as thing I yearn for come November
Snow as *every time it does, I'm afraid*
    it never will again

Wish

The wild things who live here
have laid down their bones like the black limbs of trees
into leaf litter and dirt.

Water waits on the table for spring
and the sun which cannot outrun this cold crawls along
so low in the sky it catches in the trees.

The beach freezes footprints in place.
Your mark remains for weeks on an expanse
that cannot shift under the weight.

Tracking in snow cover is simple.
No pedestrian escapes or is lost, not even songbirds,
whose claws rough the crust to crewelwork.

We learn to look that closely and who can blame us.
For days the sky has descended.
This builds character, we tell one another,

hearing the wish even as we nod or shrug.
What's to be done? We live here

And All

Scat and tracks on
the trail after the last
snow melt
        I wrap a bare hand
around the creviced bark of
a tree I think is dormant

Something cool sticks
to my palm
        Slug I think
for the split second
it takes me to stop

But it's a little amber bubble of
sap sparkling out
a fissure
        Hundreds, all down
and up the trunk to the crown

where dark not-yet-leaves
nib twigs
        My gaze lights then flies
Sap flows up from
the swollen earth

Signs

Kewee and I visit our woods. Finally
they're out from under the snow,
last year's leaves, beige and veined
and mostly whole. We're walking on

last summer. The wind blows evidence
of traffic and sandhill cranes over
river water, scrub, and downtown rooftops,
through empty twigs and into our ears.

Trucks and cars and prehistoric
bird calls ride the same wind my skin's
collecting, the wind that rattles leaves
and shivers Kewee's fur.

The sun's shining fine for winter,
so when I press my open palm against
the sunlit side of a tree trunk, it's warm.
Sap's beginning to flow. I don't see it

but I know it. Faith. People who say
they don't have any probably don't
go outside enough. You know the social
construction of all things? It can feel

like a small part of the story here,
where I've spied the baby tooth of
a fox kit in a bootprint, picked it up,
moved it to the crook of a tree,

then found it again, weeks later,
when Kewee nosed around
among the grass-covered roots
our bodies had carried us to again.

Proposal for a National Park Service Brochure

Take off your clothes
in the empty lot at a trailhead
any mountain trail will do
Let the sun pour down your back
Turn and close your eyes
Watch it pour orange
Dress for the trail, pack food, water
and leave your human noises in the car
Climb till your heart, lungs, and limbs braid
into the rope that pulls you on
Trees anchor switchbacks
Give them your hand a few times
and brush gently against plants and shrubs
Disturb no rocks
And when you return to the car
because of course you must
be glad for the seeds which having hitched rides
will drop healthy in your wake

True Story

He is standing shin deep in snow.
He has been walking for hours.
It is 16°F.
The sky is empty.
A half mile off a herd of elk
flows over the land.

He wants to be closer.
He sits down in the snow.
He is not cold.

The elk move toward him.
He stays still till he hears
hooves and snorts,
sees the steam of their breaths.

This landscape is treeless
and he is tall.
Without standing
he tucks the gun to his shoulder.
Sighting requires skill,
pulling the trigger, conviction.

He pulls it.
The walk down to the elk's body
feels like it might never end.
The rifle hangs from his shoulder,
fingerless and cooling.

The ears are larger
than he imagined,
furred, and the black nose
so recently alive
he flinches.

A steel blade gives an edge
to his arm, bloodied
to the shoulder.
Easier here in the snow wash.

As a boy he fished
green rivers,
so much green even
the air hummed.
Now his father lives
outside where
his mother died.

These dry hills release
their own river of beating hearts.
It takes hours to get the meat home,
two roundtrips by snowmobile,
then a long ride by pickup.

Self-Serve

I'm pumping self-serve under a sign
that still reads STANDARD
across the street from an old factory
almost entirely in ruins as of today.

The rubble clanks with backhoes
and wears a single peeling wall
on which has been spray painted,
CHRIST HAS RISEN FOR PEACE AND LOVE

and in the same hand AND JIMMIE HENDRIX TOO.
The misspelling's a reproach
and I envy the person releasing paint
in the middle of a night still vibrating with crickets.

Under my own hand the gas stops flowing.
I replace the nozzle in the pump,
the cap on the tank, and cross the lot
with keys in one hand, cash in the other.

The kid inside at the counter, in a room
that no longer opens into a service garage,
tells me he thinks a mall's going up.
Just what we need, another mall, I say,

though I am not *we*, and this cashier
might not be either. I can't know. He's expressionless
in the way that makes me try to hold my tongue
and glad to be pumping my own gas.

A House in the Country

Starlings, hundreds,
flew, filling the cavern
below trees before
disappearing onto
branches: all the weight
of spun sugar, you're thinking.
Well, they disturbed enough
molecules to jostle me,
half-conscious in a lawn chair
doing a crossword. Listen.
This is no exurban
pastoral: the husband
next door shot his wife in
the head. Gossips blame her
nagging, but think of
gray-wisped sweat on her cheeks
and those starlings, so many,
so light, then gone.

The Language of Field Guides

1

It's not a bad thing: this
July, gone cool and northern.

Our car furrows the water
mirages of the interstate,

and my husband guides
the steering wheel

as I've seen yearling horses
guided. He'd make love

right here on the highway
between ditches of sumac,

but I flip through radio stations
and entertain ghosts hovering

like hawks. The last spring thaw
uncovered mullein leaves, flat

rosettes the frost didn't kill.
Their yellow flowers bloom

where mullein grows best,
roadsides, construction sites,

marks of our restlessness,
waste places, say field guides.

2

In maple and cedar woods
bounded by Superior

and the Huron Mountains,
a mesh of leaves

and pure cumulus
form a piebald mirror.

I promise to return
when *scarlet drupes*

supplant *white bracts*,
as red-edged leaves

push the first snowflakes
from the clouds.

3

From the overlook, I'll watch
butterflies trail each other

up and down columns of air,
holding the sky. *Courtship flight,*

winks one naturalist. *Escape
from unwanted suitors*, winks

another, but for the butterflies
and for me, it's not just that.

Anisoptera, Florida

Dragonfly, two sets of wings
upside down, on the porch ceiling

waiting. What focus! Two days
and counting, while Claire

very old and unsteady, dangles
in a crystal box on

the other side of a condo door,
watching an osprey nest

seven floors above the suspicious
ground. Drained? Filled?

All scraped places here are barren.
Limestone, I guess but don't know.

They grow the best tomatoes
a mile down the road.

How? Sun and sun
and water piped, but soil?

Anisoptera, yes, but
not *at rest.* There's gravity, wind

hunger, thirst. And holding
Claire high, above the earth.

Another Coast

Light invades the beach at all hours
Bright highrises clasp floodlights
and other lamps
throwing shadows

as private as the pauses between
beams of searchlights
stinging gray plains of ocean
Even seashells have their skinny doubles
gridding sand then foam

If you sailed from sea at night
you could track the routes of light
to towers of masonry plastic glass
You could come ashore where waves
stay illuminated

or you could come about
and let the darkness keep you

Sand Key

I jump into a school of sergeant majors
The yellow- and black-striped disks
of their hundreds of bodies fall
rise and shatter sunlight

Gulf opens from surface to space
Barracudas hang
in the water and watch
as if it's air
and they're raptors
Perhaps they name us

Without preference
clear cold March water
buoys us all

Almost immediately I'm shivering
exaggerating strokes and kicks
to keep warm
To keep the mask sealed
I must not even grin

Who can say what a hurricane means
the one that drowned Sand Key
for instance destroying buildings and people

Every living thing is food
The rest is mystery

Some Things I Needed to Know

Rain all morning
                        heavy now
on spruce bows
                        I've been watching
the slippery elm
                        made new by
float glass and weather
                                A single bird's
silver chortle
                        returns me
to the Everglades
                        where I memorized
the voice of
                        a red-bellied woodpecker
night without
                        any light except stars
a couple of planets
                                the very marrow
Sunlight flows from
                        blue needles
and changes
                        the elm again
Painted buntings
                        Bermuda grass
The color of winter in
                                Flamingo

Report from the End of the Twentieth Century

Last night our house settled deep
into swells burnished by moonlight.

Our sleep was the sleep of mollusks.

I'm walking sidewalks imprinted
with years and hands and tracks.

Concrete ages like coral torn from the sea.

A red daylily blossom floats in
grassy leaves browning toward winter.

Rose petals fold back into hips.

One half mile below the floor of the Pacific
we detonated another atomic bomb.

Water foamed for hours at the surface.

Lake Effect

I dream of drawing trees on ivory paper, awaken
and find black night crowding
thermal windows behind thick drapes.

A few streetlights cast temporary shadows
on haunches of snow. We don't ask,
where's the sea? We can walk to it,

and to acres of scrub, pasture, crop,
asphalt draining to it, and the reactor
it cools. Here is the cup we dip hesitantly

even under the spigot. Here is the forest
where owls ride trees, wild wind rides twigs
and feathers. A leaf surfs its gully in the snow.

3

If He Could Keep Her, He Would

On his side in the sand
he watched clouds fold back from the sun.
Her fuchsia lips imparted flamboyant tattoos.
Meadow was thick in her hair
as it looped between their mouths.

She told him he couldn't
hold her tightly enough. But he tried.
So if their legs slipped between each other's
and their hips knocked bones, then held—well,

he closed his eyes.
His lashes laved sand from her forehead.
Their mouths opened to gulp each other's air.
Their tongues: mute limbs,

exchange of wet and heat,
as when doors are propped open in summer
until wind slams them shut.

Succession

Occasional clutter of his front seat, she's
talking about possibilities. He's filling a
pipe with pot and running his fingers
through his own hair, thinking: mating
shouldn't lead to this fury, the way
she quickly gets drunk and lets him have it.
Human, we do it best: pull up plants by
their roots then stuff them in landfills, a
few blossoms left to float in a bowl
on a scarred wooden table. Wildflowers
replenishing a charred mountainside
offer answers, ways of seeing and being
that affirm silver linings: the fuchsia-blue
flare of fireweed and the promise of cones.

His

hand cups the ceramic surface of his mug.
She watches the black disk of her coffee wobble
with passing trucks. Cooling molecules
contract to minimum surface area,
new tension. They sit on steel chairs,

plastic seats the size of his hand.
Their faces cling to the rims of their bodies.
She smooths an imagined tablecloth,
a bed sheet, as a smile steadies his face.
Does anybody sleep in waterbeds anymore

do you think? She spoons sugar into her coffee,
stirs. His finger traces tight and tighter circles
on the mug where steam's condensed.
On the sidewalk, slush and toddlers
in snowsuits—red, yellow, and blue.

Catalogue

Look at her, utterly
flat-footed on library tile
between card catalogue files and
plate glass windows
turned mirror by the night,

reflecting row upon row of
little wooden drawers with
tiny brass pulls and frames
holding wee paper labels
marked, for instance, Aa–Ab.

Look at the beige linoleum
so highly polished it reflects
every lettered label, and
her shadow self standing
flat-footed, imagining

she pulls *Jude the Obscure* from the
blue knapsack, tears out
a page then folds it in half,
in quarters, then eighths,
each crease seeded with words.

Look at her looking at
the card catalogue files,
imagining she curls an index
finger under one hook and
pulls a drawer open to

scores of thumbed cards,
every single one hole-punched
and slipped onto a brass rod
anchored to a drawer and
joined with a book here

under this same roof,
because capable hands with
their capable fingers once
held each book and typed
an ink record onto paper.

This is how we indexed
records of our knowledge and
this is where we arranged it.
And this is where she ran into him
finally and he ran into her,

brimming with unuttered
words and hauling a knapsack
heavy with papers and books
through the corridor between
cards and windows

reflecting the two of them standing
right where she was considering
flipping a drawer of cards
forward and dropping one
folded page into the space.

Look at her stopped, knowing
the concrete planters outside
the windows were growing
shrubs simply from dirt, and
fountain water climbed into air.

I'm noticing this from far
in the inscrutable future, because
this is where I was walking
and he was walking and
she was walking with him and

we all stopped together on
the polished linoleum in
front of the mirrored plate glass,
and rows upon rows of
card catalogue files, where my

whole body relaxed into the
same goddamned space he'd
left it in over and over.
My heart really rather
suddenly feeling like a

peony bud, my chest
too small to hold the blossom
it would become, because when
they stopped he put his hands
on her shoulders and his eyes on mine.

Look at us three, standing next to
the calling cards of countless
books, packed into dark
wooden boxes. The page from
Jude almost left in the one

that happens to be the one
that's never opened again,
my fingers already preparing
to stop a certain kind of
touching forever, alongside

an index of practically
everything important that's
already been read.

Archived

~

Margaret

(I wonder if others who appear so sensible
are as foolish as I.)

Mother sugared off this forenoon
and sent me with maple sugar to the neighbors.
Our road too muddy for the sleigh,
I walked.

I met a silly-looking man
with his hands in his pockets
and a sun-burned face.
He asked me question upon question,

beginning easily enough:
"Does your father want to hire a man?"
But then, "I suppose you are not married?"

(I am fourteen and it is the kind of weather
that always makes me feel as if I should like to go
and lie down in the sun.
The new grass is so green and soft and young.)

"No sir, not I."
"I suppose you would if you could get a chance to."
I started off.
"Whosoever lives on that farm, there,
are they looking for a hired man?"
I kept going.
"Where does this road lead to?"

(O, give me a horse
to roam through the prairie grasses
of the West
where there are no men or folks.
Let me taste something of the world.)

"I have got to deliver this sugar, sir."

~

Anne

Dear Jack,
The sky is overcast with fish-back clouds,
always a sure precursor of a storm,
I think I have told you.

We took a ride to Sylvanport and Father's mill today.
When we stopped for supper
my horse broke the strap to the wagon.
I remounted so as to teach
the naughty creature a lesson.

Back home, I get such a shaking
and rubbing down right & left.
Dr. Trine says his Swedish Movement Cure
will make me look better and behave better
(and feel better?).

There is a feeling in my bones
as though you would be in town
about the last of next week.
What do you think of my feelings
or of my bones?

By the way, coming home I led the way,
and Mr. A. did not drive fast enough
to keep up. I would walk
every ten or fifteen minutes
so he might overtake us.
I did not tell him so.

My horse and I are well suited, I think.
It is all in fun, Jack.

Emma

I am told
"Never to be
any skeletons trotted out of the closet"
So be it—I can have my thoughts
can't I?
Bells' daughter murdered and thrown in the river
and I don't care—I have my own trials.
("Emma!") Mother talked about Mr. Taylor's proposal
with such horror
that it made me feel almost distracted
She rarely attends services—Married for Gold
"What will be done when poor Emma marries the parson?"
If only I could lay bare some bones
in this book open on my lap—
but what I write is well-scrubbed
and perfumed—He is repulsive
bad teeth and three motherless children . . .
Father's Facts for Farmers *tells me*
"The art of being loved
should be the first thought of every girl"
But the Bible teaches me to do the loving
I am 26 and unmarried—proposed to
and in despair—Duty fastens my frame
I shall marry the minister
because God has it I shall
Prayed all night—Sick all yesterday
The St. Clair would have washed the flesh
from the girl's bones if they had not found the body
and the skeleton appear on some shore some time
He is a man of God and I a mere woman
Didn't I write once
"It has seemed to me that there is no position
in life that I would take such pleasure in
accepting as that
of a pastor's wife"? But this pastor?
Oh for grace! grace! grace!
such a skeleton reposes in my sorry head
God sees it—I half hope someone
will read between these lines

~

Catherine

Needlework fancywork
ball games
stayed home all day
tatting ironing visiting
fancywork concert circus
all day at home
crocheted ironed
called at Morgan's
the rink the capitol the college
home
knitting ironing
red shirtwaist
green shirtwaist
black satin shirtwaist
Cook Fair
Owosso Fair
received a letter
wrote a letter
sunny and hot
cloudy and hot
cloudy
cold
snowy
grim

Ironed napkins
Ironed napkins
Ironed napkins
What did you think about?
Ralph's predictable *"peaches, peaches,"*
sleigh-riding till 4 a.m., again,
another girlfriend lost to marriage?

Letters left to answer?
Your New Year's resolution:
Keep up with correspondence better.

Transported to *fin de siècle* Lansing
I'd want to ask you
what, after the gift diary
each Christmas,
Mrs. Van gave you
for your wedding.
The rest of the diary is blank.

~

Louise

These our dark days:
cold dripping spring, and War sits,
bird of prey above
our prairie home. Men steal and kill:
everyday affairs.
It is like burying a loved one alive
to say goodbye when they leave
for the War, sturdy inside
blue. Handsome under caps.
I'm afraid

they are not ready to die.
Souls unsaved. If they were ready,
it would not seem so bad. God,
still the wings
and seal the beak!
I hope for light.

Fathers, sons, husbands. Mine:
afraid to travel for trade.
But home. Wet and cold,
a northwest wind flaps about our cabin.
I leave the children to their naps longer
and let Henry sleep on

in this midafternoon dusk:
rain on the window
catches what little light gets through.

Mary

Cyrus disobeyed.
I tied him to the table leg.

He was anyhow but contented
& at last exclaimed,
"I don't want to be tied.
I think Indians tie dogs.
When I went to the Chief's lodge,
I think I saw his dog tied."

A while since I kissed him
after washing his face.
He asked why I do so,
adding, "Dogs kiss . . ."

He stood at the door
hallooing awhile
& then came in, wished to know
what it was he heard in the mountain.
We did not know at first,
but he added, "Cyrus knows.

We & the trees & every thing have a shadow
& it is like that I think.
My voice has a shadow."

"I don't want to say please."
"I don't want milk."
We used the rod till we feared
to longer. We kept him in bed
all day & still tried to induce him
to say please, but to no purpose.

He wanted, he said, to go out
& see the bright sun.
I regret the course we pursued.
I often fear being guilty
of the very thing for which
I punish my child.

Ways

~

She still classifies trees
good or not-good for climbing

~

Telephone wires lie across crowns
staves catching birds
as they light

~

If we get behind enough
ferns and birch trunks
the road will disappear

~

Not the chainsaw

~

They're fenced from the woods
by a row of poplars
No Hunting or Trespassing

~

Road dirt
birch bones and ash

~

A few final snow puddles
reflect wreckage of clouds

~

What kind of fool plants
pines in straight rows
God never made
woods like this

~

He grinned
She was serious

~

Look
Someone's removed the barbed wire
and signs from these fence posts

~

They're grooming this place
for a subdivision

~

The tree decided where
the road stopped
He wouldn't go around it

~

She wouldn't cut it down

Self-Defense

Ditch weed and sunlight already stripped
to gray deer hide I wore fluorescent
and kept to the road

Something motionless and white
lit the shadows in the pines
so I followed a footpath into the woods

Dun body of a whitetail
cracked ribs and a bloodless hole
black with rainwater

Dull cloud of her eye on mine
I buried her with fallen leaves

Farther North and Across a Sea

Summer, never a time of stars
for me. They show up too long
after daylight
has finally moved off
and turned about three times
in the long grass,

                    trampled
a hollow where we could sleep
or wait for sunshine's return
if we had not forgotten what
to do with night.

Once, living in winter
with freshwater seas meant
darkness so deep we could reach
into it as into soil proliferating
as if it always would.

                    Stars
were as familiar then
as weeds and far too numerous
to organize, though we tried.

For months snow fell and
muffled whatever grew.

                    Fields
collected light, as the grasses
and clover, yellow flags and
manure of Moveen must,
whether or not
we are awake.

Antivenin No. 1

I can stare the moon full in the face
all night long if I want to
Maybe I will

November 14, 2016

4

In Medias Res

All the traveling through day or dark
pursued, this song or that playing

through the essential air, shadows
crisscrossing fields and roads prettily,

moon glinting off the car's interior chrome.
This dark spangled with bling—

Spangles, the dapple-gray stallion
summer-camp girls rode through fields,

decades dead and buried.
Buried, the fervent hope, not *used*

in some unwritable way, *oh please*.
The old obsession with horses carried

right into the middle of life
upon the engineered skin of the earth

where forest has given way to field
has given way to concrete and built.

How natural it all feels, how inevitable,
until the nighttime light evokes

a ghost from the transition time,
grasses and flowers underfoot,

gray mane under hand, hair blown
back like a pennant on a pole

of a ship that sailed upon a wilderness of sea.
Cicadas for a soundtrack, and the wind.

Porch Swing

There is a bit of blue in everything
even shadows enfolding
these scraps
twigs, planks, spindles
It is all wood
and it was all sky once
At the side of the road that ends here
someone has tried to stop a tree
lopped the branches
to the first fork
New shoots, resilient as grass, pull
against the same gravity
that battens sky
among us
Everything gives back light

The Branch Might Break

March. The trees are dead.
I'm not alone in fearing this.

Last October the leaves were brilliant,
as if lit from within.
My friend, almost a father, died
in the arms of the woman
who would deliver their daughter
into the same sturdy embrace.

The branch might break.
Snagged or not, it will crumble,
into the air or earth.
So familiar, we say, mundane.

Here is why it's not.
Sap will creep.
Bark will surrender its cache.
Life will prod the living.

Fire

Our trees ignite. Every year
it happens. On another side

of the continent, it's houses
and everything within and among

that couldn't be carried
or wasn't: mattresses, blankets,

baby photos, security systems,
soil, houseplants, new leaves.

When the conflagration
ebbs, the earth will lie scorched

as winter, at least the sort
we have here, where we'll rake

and blow things on to frozen.
Snow will cover over everything

for sleep until the gray blackens
because it's soil and everything's

about to grow again. You begin
to see the limits of metaphor.

I awaken every day celebrating,
unwilling or unable to write

elegies for all the beauty we
will surely lose. There is so much

we won't, and in our desire
to appear clever and unsurprised

we might cease to see at all.
So, rather, our trees are flooded

with the same colors as always,
colors masked by summer's green

riot and the way sunlight enters
earth. Our leaves prepare to stop

being leaves but not to stop being.
Litter, then soil, then houseplants,

babies, mattresses, burglar alarms,
the impermanent confection of a house.

Memorial Service in Sanctuary Woods

The white dove flapped
light wings against the heavy
August air.
           We watched her
fly up, past the green flames
of the trees.
           Luke's mother
sobbed a sharp sob,
               and the rest of us,
hoping she had held him
for every moment of his
short life,
          breathed wood smoke, dust,
the perfume of living leaves, and
cried.
        The dove wasn't wild.
How far from home?
             Closer to
death now, creation.

One by One

Driving west through
stacked suburbs

the ones that steal starlight

the ones that grabbed
people and all the stuff
they took with them when
interstates were new and
lawns looked like salvation

We speed past
other cars and trucks

Within every one
lies a blood-warm tongue
in a warm mouth
Eyes watch
Hands steer

Feet press toward the ground
We accelerate into the dark
Toward and away

After everything
trees still rise up here by the side of the road
fiercely protective mothers and fathers

And the stars come out

Settlement

Unplowed road through
a National Tree Farm
Snowmobile that splits silence

Apple seed discarded to
a highway shoulder, flesh and
golden skin nibbled to the core

Feather beneath the head of
the one you love most, ticking
that may or may not release it

Grandchildren, children
parents, ancestors; story clipped
to the Bible family tree

In forests billions of leaves
breathe, without

Detroit

Scrub and brush
reassert grow

after so much assembly
so much undone

I learned asphalt isn't forever
He was twelve

And I was dragging
decades of concrete

behind me without even realizing—
Drop them then

Tear them up and plant
vegetables in a parking lot

Goats and chickens behind
the last house standing

Totally illegal
but no one complains

He was probably forty-something
What's there to complain about

And Eastern Market fills up with flowers
and a hundred thousand people

Lifeboat

Slipping down the Pitcher's thistle dune slope
at the edge of a freshwater sea,
I recall the lifeboat, wooden on a wooden rack, paint peeling,

there, for so many years behind the foredunes,
miles from any road in the dune-grass shade of cottonwoods,
steps from the beach,

but nearly in the woods, so who'd have been there
to see, carry, launch, paddle, rescue, in this land scrap
without sidewalks,

land where what assembles, assembles according to some
fierce green fire,
even clouds tinged green, reflecting lake

and shore, and out there: cold fresh water,
huge heavy body of it,
under condensation that's cloud, the sea in the sky.

We look up,
see doorways to space, stars, planets—Saturn, say,
which photographed in infrared looks elegant as the *Titanic*

pulling away from the White Star Dock for something
inimitable as outer space. Perhaps a child's thought,
perhaps others':

not enough lifeboats, absolutely sinkable. Surely
someone thinking: however clever, we're terrestrial
creatures who must stay warm or die.

Oh, to know the ones who took care here,
installed a lifeboat on shifting land, where
creatures that crawl and fly are sole witnesses to the vigil,

to know the purchase of their steps, the stories they told,
the things they remembered,
what they lost, and how.

Before the Snow Moon

Frozen lagoon blown clear by real wind
We simply sat on the ice to lace our skates

No matter that the enclosing dunes were modest
We were tucked in among mountains

On the other side someone's beagle wailed
from the under-reconstruction lighthouse

And the ice-cold Great Lake rolled
silent with somnolent fish

A bitter northeasterly carried highway rumble
and the opaque ice sang deeply

I set my boots on two century-old pilings
to keep them out of the snow

What ships bumped up against
the same stubs before sand filled the river mouth

What canoeists floated summer
days when the shores clicked with frogs

A bald eagle soared in from the north
My eye met the eye turned earthward

All of us flying in our separate ways through the same space
watched over by ghosts certainly

A smudge of brighter-than was a gibbous moon
The sun set without fanfare

Light damped down to nearly nothing
by ferocious cloud cover

Not five hours later
I was awakened by a great horned owl

I climbed out from under a pile of quilts
and went to the window to lift the sash

On the other side of the parking lot
pines old as the pilings held old nests up

Twigs of a young black walnut scraped the gutters
Snowflakes ticked against the glass

Cold air carried hoots and soughs across the sill
I climbed back under and kept listening

After the Flood

A harvest moon obscures stars
and makes new ones in the hoarfrost
I leave them uncharted
and step from the sidewalk
into the flood plain's mud

A few weeks into receding waters
the park is already bulldozed clear
The river's arranged itself
among riverbeds and roots

Alluvial, delta, silt
words I need to remember
arrive with the sounds of traffic
I find a stick to scratch notes
into muck nearly frozen with winter

The pen catches on acorns
clotted in tire ruts
each battered kernel holding
a tangle that might
throw out roots, branches
leaves, another constellation

When I lean into the wind it holds.

Aubade

It is good to be
mortal but otherwise flawed
to care and suffer and
look out into
the lemon light of morning and
call it beautiful and
feel expectation
for the eighteen thousandth
two hundredth and sixty-second
time

There Is Always This

Across sunrise
        branches release
                billows of green sail.
Everywhere
      the brown sketch of limbs
                  overhung by the flap of canvas:
spring, forest, olive.
        All there
          and I look,
from the one hill in town,
             watched over by a murder of crows.
The sidewalk, washed
        as if with green water,
               pulses
against the salt-beaten
        edges of lawn.
             Just yesterday
the whole world still sleeping,
        weeks of buds,
             red, mostly, and gold,
and of motion so minuscule and new
          sleep seemed like death,
                an opening.
Silver sky, not gray,
        slides among the solid birds
             lifts a few feathers
and catches the snap of sail.
        Everything touching and being
             touched.
It can happen this way,
        a whole neighborhood reanimated.
             Twigs
and last year's leaves
        gather light,
          black crows most of all,
each one pulling in rays,
        holding on.

The Old Days

The Great Lake is sound carried
over the foredunes, invisible and real as the moon.
We feel it like the promise of an acorn,
an old dog's glance back over her shoulder.

We'd walk second-growth woods, Kewee and I,
a dog and a person returned
from strange lands: chemistry-stung America, circa 1962,
where I was born,

neighbor to few birds, fewer weeds.
The trees were big and old and well trimmed,
so were the houses.
Even driveways were well scrubbed.

Most lawns didn't have down twigs.
Ours had a tunnel of vines across the back, at least,
like the ones that hang from these trees
above a duff mess.

Crows shout down from the canopy,
recalling nothing from those old days,
but I think of them
as the crows harass an owl who sits tight,

silent in her home oak.
I cannot see her, but I know she's there, like Kewee,
and the lake we can't inhabit.
These dunes a consolation.

Love, Exactly

Nearsighted child
dripping from the pool

I'd lie on the warm deck
press my ear to the concrete
watch water seep through grit
and hear waterfalls and rivers

I'd feel one with the invisible distance
and certain as with you

Beginning With My Daughter's First Word

leaf
sits
at the end
of a vascular
system that
extends without
interruption
through the twig
to which it's
attached along
successively
larger branches
through fork
after fork

down the trunk
out the main
artery of a
twisted and
bent root
to the smallest
root hair
probing the
soil for
moisture and
nutrients

as a
molecule
of water
evaporates
from the leaf
a tug is
felt at the most
distant root
tip

leaf
is one
endpoint
of a thread
that resonates
throughout
an entire
tree

NOTES ON THE POEMS

For the fictionalized voices in "Archived," I'm indebted to these late writers of diaries and letters: Isa H. Parker Smith, whose unpublished girlhood diaries, 1874–75, I discovered among her father's papers, tucked into a file folder with his name on the tab; Ella, last name unknown, whose unpublished letters, 1874–75, to Frank Harlow, I found among the Harlow family papers (I have been unable to find any other information about her); Elizabeth Gurney Taylor (diaries, 1866); Edna Haskins (diaries, 1894–95); Isa H. Parker Smith's mother, Hariette A. Johnson Parker, (diaries, 1853 and 1862). These diaries and letters are archived at the University of Michigan's Bentley Historical Library. I am also indebted to the late Mary Richardson Walker—the "Mary" section of "Archived" is comprised of passages found in Walker's diaries, 1833–47—and to editors Cathy Luchetti and Carol Olwell, who included the excerpts of Walker's diaries in *Women of the West* (St. George, UT: Antelope Island Press, 1982).

"The Branch Might Break" is dedicated to the memory of Mark Webster, and to Annie Dean and Mary Benjamin Webster.

"Memorial Service in Sanctuary Woods" is dedicated to the memory of Luke, and to Teresa, Mike, and Rose.

"My Daughter's First Word" is a found poem. The words are taken from Peter J. Marchand's book, *Autumn: A Season of Change* (Lebanon, NH: University Press of New England, 2000).

ACKNOWLEDGMENTS

I am indebted and grateful to the editors of the publications and presses named here who gave many of these poems early homes.

"Beginning With My Daughter's First Word" was published as a fine-art letterpress broadside by Lauri Taylor (Salt Lake City, UT: Loose Cannon Press, 2016).

Some of these poems appear in the chapbooks *Before the Snow Moon* and *Dog Heart* (Ann Arbor, Michigan: Alice Greene & Co., 2013 and 2011). Thank you, Jill Peek. The poems are better for your delicate editing.

"Porch Swing" was published as a hand-bound, fine-art letterpress book and broadside by Jean Buescher Bartlett (Ann Arbor, MI: Bloodroot Press, 1996).

"After the Flood," "Self-Serve," and "After Reading *The Late, Great Lakes*" were exhibited in the Midland [Michigan] Artwalk.

Atticus Review: The Rocks Issue: "Love, Exactly"

The Bonfire Review: "Self-Serve," "Porch Swing," and, under a different title, "His"

Chester H. Jones Foundation, National Poetry Competition anthology: "A House in the Country," under the title, "Textless Histories"

Driftwood Review: "Succession"

Dunes Review: "Sand Key" and "My Daughter's First Word," under a slightly different title

Huron River Review, Editor's Choice Award: "Proposal for National Park Service Brochure," "Self-Defense," and, under a different title, "The Branch Might Break"

I Stay Home: "The Language of Field Guides," Part 3, under the title "*Cornus Canadensis*"

Immigration & Justice for Our Neighbors: "The Dump at Ciudad Juárez"

Janus Head: "Catalogue"

The Michigan Poet, broadside and anthology, and *Ghost Fishing: An Eco-Justice Poetry Anthology*: "Detroit"

North American Review 299 and *Poetry in Michigan/Michigan in Poetry*: "Lifeboat"

Scintilla: "Report from the End of the Twentieth Century"

Seiche Ways: "After Reading *The Late, Great Lakes*"

Willow Springs: "If He Could Keep Her, He Would," under the title "If I Could Keep Her, I Would"

Writers Reading at Sweetwaters: "Grace"

In 2018, a travel grant from the Lynch and Sons Fund for the Arts and the generosity of Thomas Lynch and Teresa Scollon allowed me to spend ten days in Moveen, County Claire, Ireland, rambling and writing.

In 2008, the gift of a two-week residency at the Mesa Refuge in Pointe Reyes Station, California, gave me a room of my own, the company of kindred spirits, Deborah Richie Oberbillig and Amy Lou Jenkins, and time to explore Point Reyes National Seashore and write.

Every poem I have ever written owes some bit of its existence to four grand peninsulas: Michigan's upper and lower, South Florida, and the Pacific Northwest's Olympic. These poems are my small offering to these lands, the waters that shape them, and especially their more-than-human inhabitants. Thank you also to human beings everywhere who work to protect Earth.

The English departments at the University of Michigan and at Michigan State University nurtured my earliest poems while fueling my love of literary art. The Institute of the Environment and Sustainability at Western Michigan University and the Association for the Study of Literature and the Environment have given me academic homes. Thank you to the dedicated people who make such invaluable institutions possible, especially my classmates, colleagues, students, and the many organizations that have invited me over the years to read poems and lead workshops.

Dancer, choreographer, and Great Lakes advocate Sylvia Jania and Lakes advocate and poet Gary Schils introduced me to the joy of collaborating with dancers (Hannah, Ben) and musicians (Linda, Dale, Maureen, and Bill). Our Harbor Springs, Michigan, Celebration of Water infused me with gratitude and hope.

I am grateful indeed for the support my poem making has received over the decades from all my teachers and colleagues, especially Charles Baxter,

Alice Fulton, Mary Ruefle, Richard Tillinghast, my MFA cohort, Diane Wakoski, and Albert "Bud" Drake. For helping to usher many of the poems in this book into the world, special thanks are due Holly Wren Spaulding and Poetry Boot Camp, and Jack Ridl and the Landscapes crew; Jane Hirshfield, Marianne Boruch, Donovan Hohn, Ross Gay, and everyone at the Bear River Writers' Conference; and Ray McDaniel, Sarah Messer, and Ellen Stone. For steadfast support of my literary life over many years, my deep gratitude to poets Dan Gerber, David Swan, Keith Taylor, and Libby Wagner.

To everyone at Wayne State University Press, especially M. L. Liebler, Michael Delp, Annie Martin, Carrie Teefey, Emily Nowak, Kristina Stonehill, and Jamie Jones, from the bottom of my heart, thank you. Jen Anderson, I could not have asked for a more skillful copyedit. Nancy Mitchnick, I adore your paintings; thank you for sharing *Ocean View*. Katrina Noble, I love the cover.

To my friends and family, you are priceless to me. Thank you for not just tolerating but for aiding and abetting my poem making. Know that, for better or worse, you have helped make this little book possible.

Sophie, this book is for you. May you never stop creating. May you fall back in love with this crazy beautiful world every day. David, you know . . .

ABOUT THE AUTHOR

Born in the Great Lakes basin, Alison Swan is a Mesa Refuge alum and a Petoskey Prize for Grassroots Environmental Leadership co-winner. Her poems and environmental writing have appeared in two chapbooks and in many anthologies and journals. She teaches at Western Michigan University and lives in the Huron and Kalamazoo River watersheds. Her edited volume, *Fresh Water*, was named a Michigan Notable Book.

CPSIA information can be obtained
at www.ICGtesting.com
Printed in the USA
JSHW020426170622
27133JS00004B/12